A Guide for Using

The Very Hungry Caterpillar

in the Classroom

Based on the book written by Eric Carle

*This guide written by **Barbara Shilling***

Teacher Created Materials, Inc.
6421 Industry Way
Westminster, CA 92683
www.teachercreated.com

©1999 Teacher Created Materials, Inc.
Reprinted, 2000

Made in U.S.A.

ISBN 1-57690-335-4

Contributing Editor
Dona Herweck Rice

Illustrated by
Wendy Chang

Cover Art by
Dennis Carmichael

Table of Contents

Introduction and Sample Lessons

A good book can touch the lives of children like a good friend. Great care has been taken in selecting the books and activities featured in the Literature Unit series. All the activities are intended for use with primary students, grades 1–3. Some activities may need to be modified to meet the needs of students at various levels of ability. (Several modification options are included in Suggestions for Using the Unit Activities, pages 7–13.) Activities in all academic subjects have been incorporated to make this a unit which teaches and reinforces skills across the curriculum. It is hoped that students will enjoy the story while gaining knowledge and skills in all areas.

Teachers who use the activities to supplement their own ideas can follow one of the following methods.

Sample Lesson Plan

The sample lesson plan on page 4 provides you with a specific set of introductory lesson plan suggestions for *The Very Hungry Caterpillar*. Each of the lessons can take from one to several days to complete and can include all or some of the suggested activities. Refer to Suggestions for Using the Unit Activities for information relating to the unit activities.

Unit Planner

If you wish to tailor the suggestions on pages 7–13 to a format other than the one prescribed, a blank Unit Planner is provided on page 5. On a specific day, you may choose activities you wish to include by writing the activity number or a brief notation about the lesson in the Unit Activities section. Space has also been provided for reminders, comments, and other pertinent information related to each day's activities. Reproduce copies of the Unit Planner as needed.

Sample Lesson Plan

Lesson 1

- Introduce the unit by using any or all of the Before the Book activities (page 7).

- Read About the Author (page 6) with the students to learn interesting facts about the author and other books by Eric Carle.

- Introduce the vocabulary (page 7, activity 2).

- Read the story.

- Complete the Story Comprehension activity (page 29).

Lesson 2

- Instruct the students to read the story aloud with a partner.

- Discuss some of the Story Questions (page 21).

- Use the Sentence Strip Frames (page 18) and stick puppets (pages 22–24) to recreate the story.

- Reinforce the new vocabulary with Word Cards (pages 19–20), The Long and the Short of It (page 27), Word Fun (page 28), Number Words and Booklet (pages 33–35) and Hungry for Words (page 41).

Lesson 3

- Reinforce fine motor skills by completing the Metamorphosis Maze (page 40).

- Let the students use their imaginations with Imagine (page 26) and Cocooning (page 30).

- Continue discussing the Story Questions (page 21).

- Create a story web for the book (page 10).

- Continue the vocabulary activities (page 7, activity 2).

Lesson 4

- Reread the story. Discuss stages of development from caterpillar to butterfly and complete Birth of a Butterfly (page 36).

- Practice writing skills and foster creativity with a writing activity (page 25).

- Continue discussing the Story Questions (page 21).

- Learn about the parts of a caterpillar (page 39).

- Continue the vocabulary activities (page 7, activity 2).

Lesson 5

- Develop a unit on nutrition with Sorting Saturday (page 32) and The Very Healthy Caterpillar (pages 37–38).

- Complete Fruity Math (page 31).

- Complete the Story Questions (page 21).

- Continue to practice writing skills and foster creativity with a writing activity (page 25).

Lesson 6

- Compare the book to other works by Eric Carle.

- Do an art activity in the style of Eric Carle. Use colored tissue paper, liquid starch, and crayons or markers.

- Enjoy playing *The Very Hungry Caterpillar* Board Game (pages 42–43).

- Write an original story (page 45).

- Have students work on center activities (pages 12 and 44).

- Host a Caterpillar Feast (page 46).

Unit Planner

Unit Activities

Date:

Unit Activities

Date:

Notes:

Unit Activities

Date:

Unit Activities

Date:

Notes:

Unit Activities

Date:

Unit Activities

Date:

Notes:

Notes:

Getting to Know the Book and the Author

Book Summary

(Available in Canada, Scholastic; UK, Scholastic Limited; AUS, Ashton Scholastic Party Limited)

This beautifully illustrated and whimsical story details the life cycle of a newly hatched caterpillar, small in size but with an enormous appetite. The reader will delight in the antics of the caterpillar as he eats a variety of colorful foods each day, including such natural foods as pears, plums, and strawberries. However, this caterpillar is so hungry that he does not stop there. He continues to eat everything in sight, including chocolate cake, salami, and an ice-cream cone. As he eats, he leaves holes in the book's pages. It is no surprise that he ends up with a terrible stomachache. Thankfully, the caterpillar finally comes to his senses and returns to eating leaves. At this point, he forms a cocoon and undergoes his transformation into a brilliant butterfly.

The book is illustrated with Carle's characteristic collages in bright and dazzling hues. The lines are simple, childlike, and as engaging as the story itself. It is clear why the book has become a children's classic.

About the Author

Eric Carle was born on June 25, 1929, in Syracuse, New York. His interest in art began at an early age. He remembered painting in kindergarten on large sheets of paper with bright colors and wide brushes. His delight with creating bright and colorful illustrations may have begun with those happy kindergarten experiences.

After working for years as a designer and art director, Eric Carle decided to become a freelance artist. An interest in children's literature blossomed when he agreed to illustrate books written by the popular children's author Bill Martin.

Joy is evident in Carle's books in the bold, bright colors, original art techniques, lively animals, playful details, and clever paper engineering. For example, a child's finger can trace the raised spider's web in *The Very Busy Spider*, and the pages grow in size with the illustrated animals encountered by *The Grouchy Ladybug*. These are just two of the many examples of Carle's ability to make books that transition from toys to literature. Consequently, reading and learning become even more enjoyable than they naturally are.

Eric Carle explains, "I would like to make childhood something special and joyous, something that the child does not want to get over with fast, something that immunizes him from such warnings as 'time to grow up,' 'be mature,' and 'don't act like a child.'" Eric Carle has done just that, as his many awards and honors make evident.

Suggestions for Using the Unit Activities

Use some or all of the following suggestions to help children understand and appreciate the story, as well as to introduce, reinforce, and extend skills across the curriculum. The suggested activities have been divided into three sections to assist the teacher in planning the unit.

The sections are as follows:

- Before the Book includes suggestions for preparing the classroom environment and the students for the literature to be read.
- Into the Book has activities that focus on the book's content, characters, theme, etc.
- After the Book extends the reader's enjoyment of the book.

Before the Book

1. Refer to *The Very Hungry Caterpillar* and other Eric Carle books (such as *The Grouchy Ladybug* and *The Very Busy Spider*) as well as nonfiction books about insects. With these books, explore the following themes:
    - characteristics of insects and arachnids
    - life cycles of insects
    - patterning
2. Introduce the vocabulary (page 14) to the students by doing any of the following:
    - Duplicate the vocabulary list for each student. Read it together orally.
    - Discuss the meanings of the words before reading the book.
    - Make several copies of the leaf pattern on page 17. Write the vocabulary words on the leaves. Display the leaves in a pocket chart. (See page 15 for directions on making a pocket chart.)
    - Make a transparency of the vocabulary page and project it for the entire class to view.
    - Print the words on chart paper.
    - Many of the vocabulary words are too difficult to become sight words for young students. However, if children are introduced to them and become familiar with the story by hearing and reading it several times, they will be able to read most of these words in context and may even add a few to their sight word vocabulary. You may also want to isolate from the story some sight words that you wish to stress at the time you are teaching this unit.
    - Complete the word search puzzle (page 41).
3. Tap into the students' prior knowledge with a discussion on times when they ate too much or felt very hungry. Talk about how "hungry" and "too full" feel.
4. Also engage prior knowledge and oral language skills by asking children to identify or recall any insects they have seen. Show pictures of insects in order to create added enthusiasm.
5. Ask students to list foods in two categories: healthful and snack or "junk" food. Talk about the differences between the two. Include the foods on the word cards (pages 19 and 20).
6. Show students the book cover. Discuss the title and picture. Make predictions.
7. Ask the students if they know other Eric Carle books. Let them tell about the books.

Suggestions for Using the Unit Activities *(cont.)*

Into the Book

1. Read the story aloud to discover what happens to the caterpillar. Stop at strategic points and have them predict what will happen next, such as when the caterpillar first hatches, when he eats five oranges and is still hungry, or after he builds his cocoon.

2. Reread the story and have the children repeat the recurring phrases.

3. Complete the Story Comprehension activity (page 29).

4. Prepare flash cards to study the days of the week. Have the children place the days in alphabetical order.

5. Assist the children in completing Word Fun (page 28).

6. Fill in the Sentence Strip Frames (page 18) with sentences or words from the story. Allow children to retell the story with the sentence strips. Use the strips for various reading activities from word recognition to capitalization and punctuation.

7. Rewrite the story on the sentence strips. Pass out the strips to individual students in random order. Have volunteers arrange the strips one at a time in sequential order. Afterwards, you may choose to leave these strips in the Hungry Caterpillar Center for individual use. (See pages 12 and 44 for more center activities.)

8. Use the questions on page 21 to check understanding of the story and to encourage discussion.

9. Cut out the pictures of the story items on pages 23 and 24. Mount them on tagboard or index cards and laminate. Reproduce several copies of the Word Cards (pages 19–20). Cut, mount, and laminate the word cards. (**Note:** Larva is not a word used in *The Very Hungry Caterpillar;* however, it is a useful word to learn in connection with the other important words in the story.) Place the item pictures in a pocket chart. Have individual students place appropriate cards next to the corresponding items. Ask them to support these label choices with evidence from the story.

   Discuss the similarities and differences among the items. This may also be a good time to introduce or review the concept of adjectives.

10. Use the puppets and theater information (pages 22–24) to retell the story. This is an excellent small group activity.

11. The journal and writing suggestions on page 25 can be done individually, with partners or small groups, or as a whole class. You may want to duplicate some stationery with characters/items from the story drawn on it for the students to write on. Include this paper in your Hungry Caterpillar Centers.

12. Review the various foods that the caterpillar eats each day. Assist the children in completing the Imagine activity (page 26).

Suggestions for Using the Unit Activities *(cont.)*

Into the Book *(cont.)*

13. The Long and the Short of It (page 27) uses vocabulary from the book to foster various language arts skills. Complete it individually or in small groups.

14. Discuss the life cycle of a caterpillar. Have the children complete Birth of a Butterfly (page 36) and Metamorphosis Maze (page 40).

15. Review the sequence of the life cycle of a caterpillar. Discuss the cocoon stage. Ask the children how they think the caterpillar would feel inside the cocoon. Have the children complete Cocooning (page 30), either independently or in pairs, as a one-day project or over a period of days.

16. Reinforce addition and subtraction skills using real fruit, and then assist the children in completing Fruity Math (page 31). After completing the activity, make a fruit salad with the children and eat it for a snack!

17. Instruct the students to color and complete the Number Words and Booklet activity (pages 33–35). Use these to learn and reinforce number words, sequence, and ordering.

18. Proper nutrition is important for both people and insects alike! Discuss and list healthful and unhealthful foods. Make headings for each food group and list foods that belong under each column. Assist the children in completing Sorting Saturday (page 32).

19. Continue the study of nutrition by having the students design a healthful diet for themselves. Assist them in incorporating all food groups when completing page 37.

20. As a class, create a healthful meal menu and then prepare it to enjoy together and/or to treat another class.

21. Expand the unit by exploring two other books by Eric Carle, *The Grouchy Ladybug* and *The Very Busy Spider*. Expand vocabulary by introducing the term arachnid. Discuss the differences between insects and arachnids.

22. Introduce literary analysis by finding similarities between the above-named books, both in style and illustration. Use Venn diagrams to make your comparisons.

The Very Hungry Caterpillar   **both**   **The Very Busy Spider**

Suggestions for Using the Unit
Activities *(cont.)*

Into the Book *(cont.)*

23. If students are unfamiliar with story webs, explain how they are used. Model a cause-effect story web for the class. Have students make a story web to check their understanding of cause and effect in the story. The story webs can be used as prewriting activities and/or to check application skills. These activities may be done individually, in small groups, or as a whole class. You may want to make a transparency for use with the entire class.

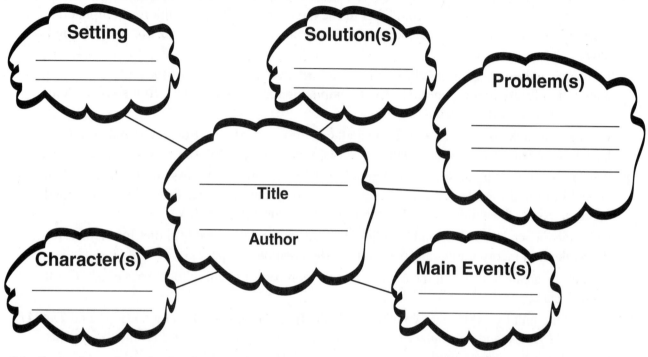

24. Several words in the book are multisyllabic. Let the students practice their syllabication skills by writing each syllable of a word in a different section of a hungry caterpillar.

25. Learn about the parts of a caterpillar. Read aloud the following directions to the students. Provide each student a copy of page 39 and a crayon. Ask them to follow the directions.

   • A caterpillar has six eyes on each side of its head. Draw five more small eyes in the first section near the front of your caterpillar.

   • Caterpillars have twelve sections. Write the numbers from one to twelve, one number in each section, starting with number one after the head. (Do not count where the eyes are!)

   • A caterpillar has legs and prolegs. Color all the legs black. (They are the ones near the front.)

   • A caterpillar is furry. Draw some brown fur along the top of your caterpillar's body.

   • Some caterpillars have black and yellow stripes as a warning to birds that they are poisonous. Make black and yellow stripes on your caterpillar's body.

   • Draw a leaf under your caterpillar. Make the leaf look as if your caterpillar has been eating it.

   • Write your name near the front end of your caterpillar's body.

26. Teach the students proper terminology. For example, what we commonly call a caterpillar cocoon is technically a chrysalis.

Suggestions for Using the Unit Activities *(cont.)*

After the Book

1. Following the suggestions and directions provided, prepare the stick puppet theater (page 22). Allow the students to construct the puppets (pages 23 and 24) by coloring and cutting out the puppets and gluing them to craft sticks. Allow small groups to reenact the book with the puppets. Use the book for your script.

2. Play *The Very Hungry Caterpillar* Board Game (pages 42–43) to reinforce the story. To play, you will need a penny and four chenille stick pieces (one red, one orange, one yellow, and one purple, each cut about 1" or 2.5 cm long). Two to four children can play at one time. Each child will choose a chenille stick. This is his or her caterpillar playing piece. Players start at the "Pop! You are hatched" space. One player at a time flips the penny. "Heads" mean go forward one space, while "tails" mean go forward two spaces. Additional directions are on the game board. Each player takes one turn at a time, unless otherwise directed. The first player to reach "Congratulations! You are a butterfly" is the winner.

3. Have the children go on a caterpillar hunt, keeping the insects in jars in the classroom. Chart the caterpillars' progress on graphs. Also collect other insects for observation.

   Additionally, you can take a nature hike/scavenger hunt. Divide the pupils into two or three groups. Give each group an identical list of nature items (twig, rock, blade of grass, soil, green leaf, yellow leaf, orange leaf, brown leaf, seed, flower, caterpillar, ant, etc.). The group with the most items on the list wins. (**Note:** Be sure that if they are to collect living things such as caterpillars and ants, that they do so carefully and in reticules designed for bug collecting and observation. After the hunt, return the bugs to the wild where they were found.)

4. Make tissue paper butterflies. Children can paint on one side of a large sheet of tissue paper. They then fold the paper. When they open it, they will have a mirror image. When dry, scrunch the paper in the middle and wrap it with a pipe cleaner. (See center activities, page 12, for a more detailed variation on this activity.)

5. Make egg carton caterpillars, using egg cartons cut lengthwise. The children can paint each section and decorate it with googlie eyes and pipe cleaners.

6. Research caterpillars, insects, and arachnids on the Internet. As well as gleaning information from the Internet, a tangible comparison can be made as to how the Internet is like a spider's web.

7. Let the children write original stories, using the beginning of *The Very Hungry Caterpillar*, but branching out into their own versions. Encourage their creativity and unique authorship. Instruct them that the more they diverge from Carle's story, the better.

   This may prove an excellent opportunity to teach or reinforce the elements of a story. (See also the story map directions on page 10.) Tell the students that their stories must have setting, character, one or more problems, and one or more solutions. Without these elements, they cannot have a story. To illustrate, provide examples of classic stories without one of the primary elements. For example, tell them the "story" of *Cinderella* without any problem to overcome, delete the solution from *The Three Pigs*, or take the setting out of *The Jungle Book*. The students will easily see how all sense of story evaporates without these important elements.

Suggestions for Using the Unit
Activities *(cont.)*

After the Book *(cont.)*

8. The Hungry Caterpillar Centers can be set up at a desk or table for students to do during free time. Make your own center sign or copy page 13 on index paper. Color the sign and laminate it, if desired. Display the sign at the Hungry Caterpillar Centers. Also prepare activity cards. To do so, reproduce page 44 onto index paper and cut out the cards, or reproduce the page on copier paper and glue each activity on an index card. Laminate the cards for durability. You will want to have writing paper and drawing paper available at the center. You may also want to set up some of Eric Carle's other books. Place these and other possible activities from the unit that adapt well to centers in the Hungry Caterpillar Centers. Students can work at the center or take work to their seats to complete it.

Here are some center ideas.

- **Sponge-Paint Butterflies:** Supply each student with a 3" (7.5 cm) tagboard circle. The student traces the circle onto a variety of colored construction paper. The child then cuts out 13 circles and glues them together in one long length. Decorate the end circle with a face. Add antennae cut out of black construction paper. Sponge-paint the colored circles of the caterpillar's body. For the wings, sponge-paint a halfsheet of colored tissue and let it dry. Fold the tissue back and forth into a fan. Cut off each of the ends of the fan at an angle. Tie a piece of string around the center of the fan. Spread the fan out on both sides. Tape or glue the wings behind the butterfly body.

- **Caterpillar Observations:** Place some live caterpillars in a ventilated jar for a day or two of classroom observation. Provide caterpillar information for the class, including books, magazines, and other reference materials. Also provide magnifying glasses to observe the caterpillars in detail. Be sure the caterpillars have food, air, and water, as needed. (See your reference materials for information on the care of caterpillars. Another excellent source for the care of most bugs—and even the acquisition of live bugs—is the company called Insect Lore. They can be reached at 1-800-LIVE-BUG.)

- **Memory Game:** Small groups of students (two to five) can play this game. Students take turns, one at a time, stating what the caterpillar might eat. They make up the foods according to the letters of the alphabet. The first player may say, "The Very Hungry Caterpillar ate an apple." The next player may say, "The Very Hungry Caterpillar ate an apple and a banana." The third player adds a *c* food and so on through the alphabet. Each player must name the foods that came before as well as his or her new food. If desired, have one student record the new foods as they are added; however, among the group the students will usually be able to recollect all items.

- **Waxed Nature Collections:** Gather small colored leaves, flattened flowers, blades of grass, etc. Place the objects on a sheet of waxed paper in an organized and attractive arrangement. Add a construction paper caterpillar, if desired. Place another sheet of waxed paper on top of the collection. Iron these objects between the two sheets of waxed paper. (**Note:** The ironing should be done by an adult aide or with adult supervision.)

Suggestions for Using the Unit Activities *(cont.)*

After the Book *(cont.)*

Hungry Caterpillar Centers

Vocabulary List

Teacher Note: See page 7 for directions.

apple
beautiful
butterfly
caterpillar
cherry pie
chocolate cake
cocoon
cupcake
hungry
ice cream
lollipop
nibbled
oranges
pears
pickle
plums
salami
sausage
stomachache
strawberries
Swiss cheese
watermelon

Pocket Chart Activities

Prepare a pocket chart for storing and using vocabulary cards, story question cards, and sentence strips.

How to Make a Pocket Chart

If a commercial pocket chart is unavailable, you can make a pocket chart if you have access to a laminator. Begin by laminating a 24" x 36" (60 cm x 90 cm) piece of colored tagboard. Run about 20" (50 cm) of additional plastic. To make nine pockets, cut the clear plastic into nine equal strips. Space the strips equally down the 36" (90 cm) length of the tagboard. Attach each strip with cellophane tape along the sides and bottom. This will hold the sentence strips, word cards, etc., and can be displayed in a learning center or mounted on a chalk tray for use with a group. A sample chart is provided below.

How to Use the Pocket Chart

1. Reproduce the patterns on page 17 onto index paper. Make vocabulary cards or sentence strips as directed on pages 7 and 8. Print the definitions or sentences on the sentence strips for a matching activity.

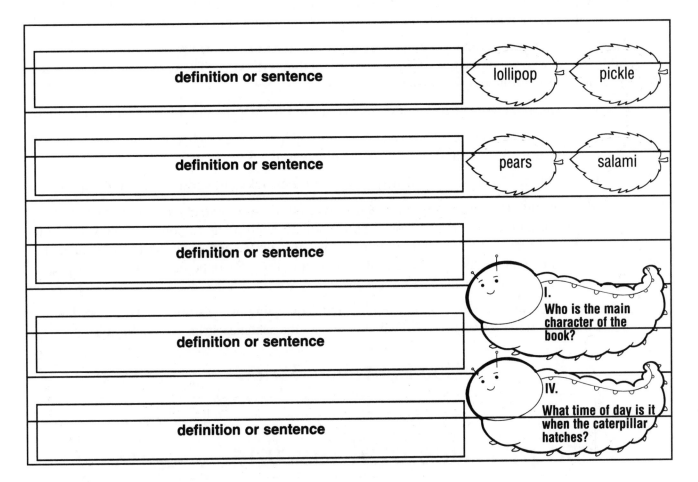

Note: The pocket chart patterns can also be used to make awards and incentives such as "Very Hungry Reader" or "Butterfly in the Making."

Pocket Chart Activities *(cont.)*

How to Use the Pocket Chart *(cont.)*

2. Reproduce several copies of the caterpillar pattern (page 17) on six different colors of construction paper. Use a different paper color to represent each of Bloom's Levels of Learning. For example:

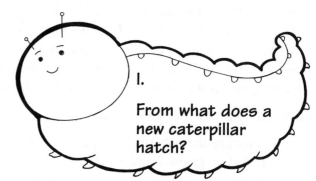

I. Knowledge *(red)*

II. Comprehension *(orange)*

III. Application *(yellow)*

IV. Analysis *(green)*

V. Synthesis *(blue)*

VI. Evaluation *(violet)*

I.

From what does a new caterpillar hatch?

Write a story question from page 21 on the appropriate color-coded caterpillar pattern. Write the level of the question and the question on the caterpillar, as shown in the example.

Use the cards after the corresponding pages have been read to provide opportunities for the children to develop and practice higher-level critical thinking skills. The cards can be used with some or all of the following activities:

- Use a specific color-coded set of cards to question students at a particular level of learning.

- Have a child choose a card and read it aloud or give it to the teacher to read aloud. The child answers the questions or calls on a volunteer to answer it.

- Pair children. The teacher reads a question. Partners take turns responding to the question.

- Play a game. Divide the class into teams. Ask for a response to a question written on one of the question cards. Teams score a point for each appropriate response. If question cards have been prepared for several different stories, mix up the cards and ask team members to respond by naming the story that relates to the question. Extra points can be rewarded if a team member answers the questions as well.

3. Use the sentence strips to practice oral reading and sequencing of the story events. Reproduce page 18, filling in the sentences. If possible, laminate the sentence strips for durability.

Use Sentence Strips

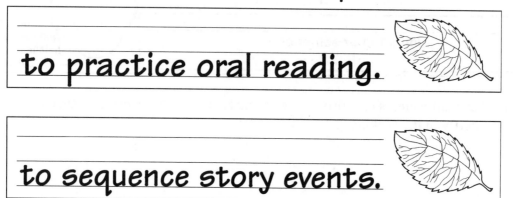

to practice oral reading.

to sequence story events.

Pocket Chart Patterns

Teacher Note: See pages 7, 15, and 16 for directions.

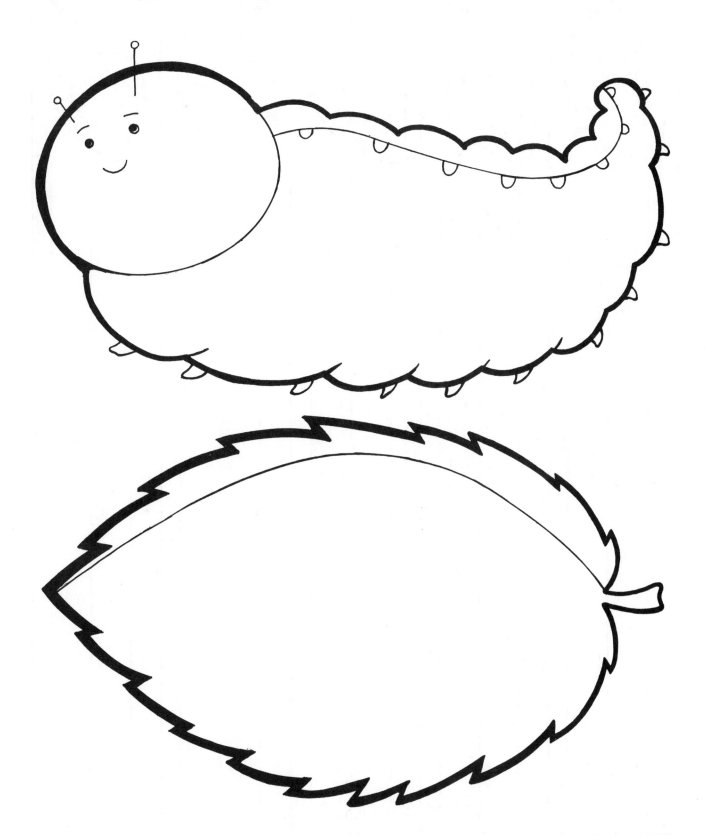

Sentence Strip Frames

Word Cards

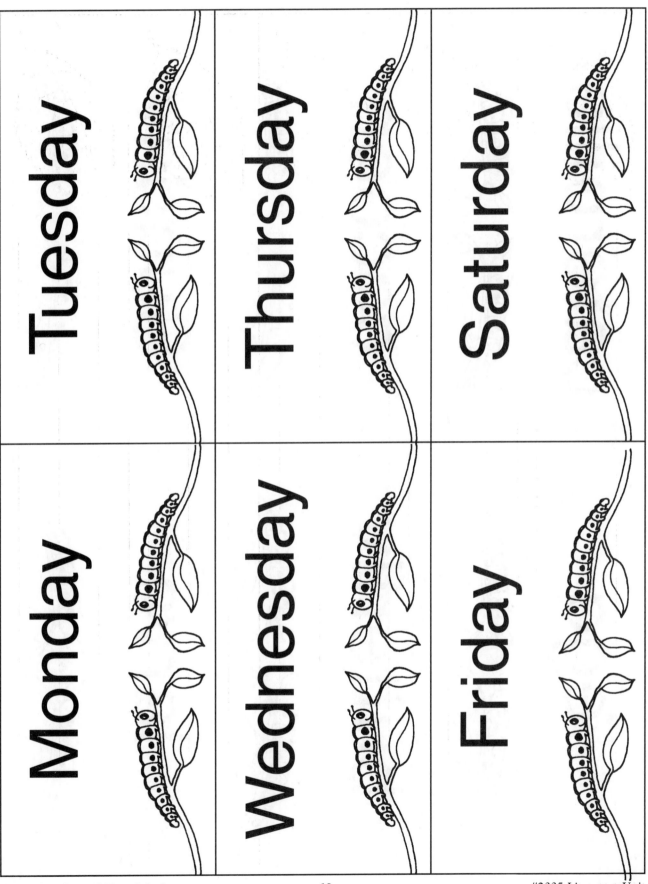

Word Cards *(cont.)*

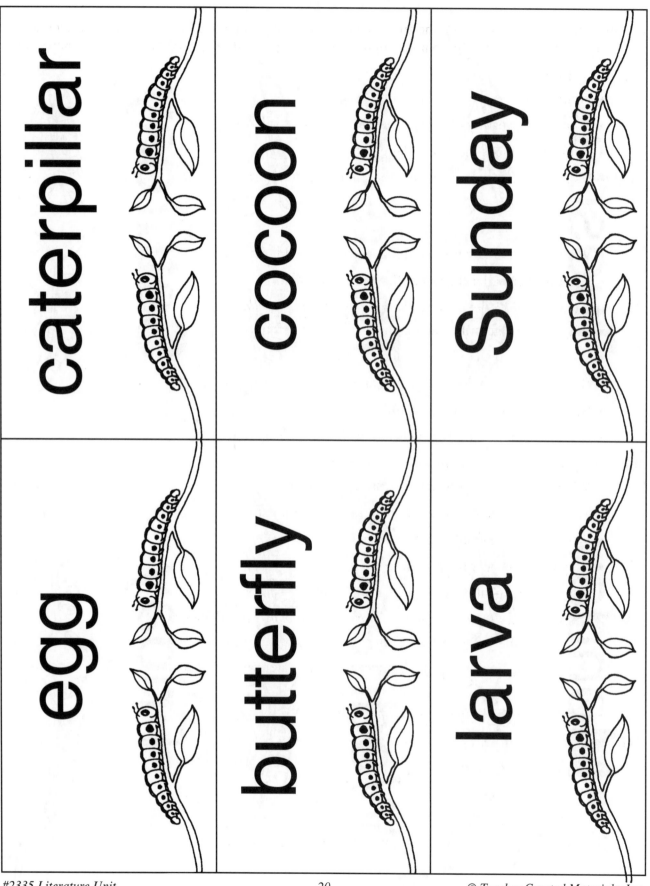

caterpillar

cocoon

Sunday

egg

butterfly

larva

Story Questions

Use the following questions with the suggested activities on pages 8 and 16. Prepare the caterpillar pattern (page 17) and write different questions from the appropriate chapters on the pattern shapes.

I. **Knowledge** (*ability to recall information*)

- From what does the new caterpillar hatch?

- What is the weather like when the caterpillar first hatches?

- Name three foods the caterpillar eats.

- Name three days on which the caterpillar eats more than one item.

II. **Comprehension** (*basic understanding of information*)

- Who is the main character of the book?

- What happens when the caterpillar eats too much junk food?

- What happens after the caterpillar forms a cocoon?

III. **Application** (*ability to do something new with the information*)

- Why must a caterpillar eat a great deal of food before entering its cocoon?

- What would you do if you ate too much?

- How do you know when you are hungry?

- Name three foods that are healthful for you to eat.

- Name three things that are unhealthful for you to eat.

IV. **Analysis** (*ability to examine the parts of a whole*)

- What time of day is it when the caterpillar hatches?

- What item is the most healthful one for the caterpillar to eat?

- Why does the caterpillar get a stomachache?

- Why does the caterpillar get fat?

- Why is there a butterfly at the end of the story?

V. **Synthesis** (*ability to bring together information to make something new*)

- What do you think would have happened if the caterpillar had eaten only leaves?

- What do you think would have happened if the caterpillar had a mother and father to show it what to do?

- What do you think the butterfly might do next?

VI. **Evaluation** (*ability to form and defend an opinion*)

- Should we feed "people" food to caterpillars? Why or why not?

- How does food affect the health of a living thing?

- What is the best part of the story? Why?

- What do you think the butterfly will do the next time it sees a pickle or salami?

Stick Puppet Theater

Make a class set of puppet theaters (one for each student) or make one theater for every two to four students. The patterns and directions for making the stick puppets are on pages 23 and 24.

Materials:

- 24" x 36" (60 cm x 90 cm) pieces of colored poster board or cardboard (enough for each student or group of students)
- markers, crayons, or paints and paintbrushes
- scissors or a craft knife (knife for adult use only)

Directions:

1. Fold the poster board or cardboard about 8" (20 cm) in from each of the shorter sides.
2. Cut a "window" in the front panel, large enough to accommodate two or three stick puppets.
3. Let the children personalize and decorate their own theaters.
4. Laminate the stick puppet theaters to make them more durable. You may wish to send the theaters home at the end of the year or save them to use year after year.

Using the Puppets and Theaters

Prepare the stick puppets, using the directions on page 23. Write a script (with your class, if desired) for *The Very Hungry Caterpillar* and use the stick puppets and theater to perform the play. (Let small groups of students take turns reading the parts and using the stick puppets.)

Let the students experiment with the puppets when retelling the book.

Have students create a new adventure for *The Very Hungry Caterpillar*, using the puppets and puppet theaters to tell their stories.

If other characters are needed, have students make their own puppets, following the directions on page 23.

Stick Puppet Theater *(cont.)*

Directions: Reproduce the patterns (pages 23–24) onto tagboard or construction paper. Allow students to color the patterns. Cut them along the dashed lines. To complete the stick puppets, glue each pattern to a craft stick. Use the stick puppets with the puppet theaters (page 22), for the activities described on page 8 or as part of your culminating experience.

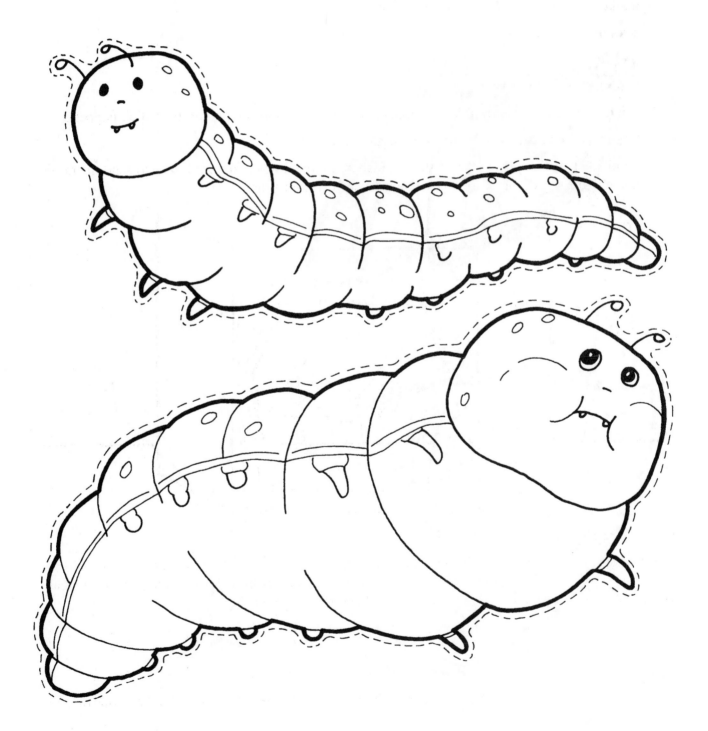

Stick Puppet Theater *(cont.)*

Journal and Creative Writing Ideas

Here are some ideas you may wish to use in your journals or for other creative writing activities. You may be asked to write on your own or complete a writing activity by working in pairs, small groups, or as a whole class.

- Every time the caterpillar bites into a food other than leaves, it magically changes into another creature. Write what happens.

- Imagine that the caterpillar meets another bug who becomes its best friend. Create a story web to prepare an original story about the caterpillar and its new friend.

- Imagine that the caterpillar is allergic to leaves. Write about what happens and how the caterpillar solves its problem.

- Write about a scary adventure when the caterpillar meets a very hungry bird.

- Pretend that the caterpillar is now living in a glass jar in your classroom. Write about its experiences from the caterpillar's point of view.

- Write a new story. Choose one of these titles: "The Very Bashful Caterpillar," "The Very Lazy Caterpillar," "The Very Confused Caterpillar," or "The Very Old Caterpillar."

- Imagine you wake up one morning on a leaf and are the size of a caterpillar. What happens?

- The caterpillar has eaten too much and decides to exercise. Describe its exercise routine.

Imagine

Imagine that you are a very hungry caterpillar. On which 10 foods do you want to nibble?

_____   _____   _____

_____   _____   _____

_____   _____   _____

_____

Draw a picture of yourself as a very hungry caterpillar eating through your chosen foods.

The Long and the Short of It

Follow the directions to find the longest, shortest, and same-size words.

1. Circle the longest word.

   caterpillar　　　　　hungry

   very　　　　　　　　chocolate

2. Circle the shortest word.

   Wednesday　　　　　cocoon

   egg　　　　　　　　leaf

3. Circle the three words that have the same number of letters.

   Monday　　　　　　Thursday　　　　　　Saturday

   Tuesday　　　　　　Friday　　　　　　　Sunday

   Wednesday

4. Which day of the week is the longest word?

5. Write two foods that have the same number of letters next to each food item below. The first one has been done for you.

   apple _berry_____　　　_____pizza_____

   plum _____　　　_____

   orange _____　　　_____

   pickle _____　　　_____

   pie _____　　　_____

Word Fun

I. Rewrite the following groups of words in alphabetical order.

1. lollipop _____

   cupcake _____

   pickle _____

2. watermelon _____

   caterpillar _____

   ate _____

3. Thursday _____

   Friday _____

   Saturday _____

4. cocoon _____

   caterpillar _____

   cupcake _____

II. Unscramble the following words.

1. uassgea _____

2. lipalrcrtea _____

3. ooccno _____

4. ghnryu _____

5. ftburtyle _____

III. Use the letters in caterpillar to spell at least five other words.

_____   _____   _____

_____   _____   _____

_____   _____   _____

_____   _____   _____

Story Comprehension

Fill in the blanks, using the words from the list below.

1. One morning, the_____sun came up, and out of

   an_____came a tiny_____.

2. On_____he ate through one_____,

   but he was still_____.

3. On Friday he ate_____oranges.

4. On Saturday_____he had a_____.

5. He built a small house called a_____.

6. He stayed inside for more than_____weeks.

7. He nibbled a_____in the cocoon.

8. He had become a beautiful_____.

apple	hungry
butterfly	Monday
caterpillar	night
cocoon	stomachache
egg	two
five	warm
hole	

Cocooning

Pretend you are a caterpillar about to become a butterfly. Write journal entries about how you feel inside your cocoon.

My Caterpillar Journal

Week 1	Week 2
Sunday	Sunday
Monday	Monday
Tuesday	Tuesday
Wednesday	Wednesday
Thursday	Thursday
Friday	Friday
Saturday	Saturday

Fruity Math

Use the chart below to solve the math problems. An example has been done for you.

Monday =	🍎	**(1)**
Tuesday =	🍐 🍐	**(2)**
Wednesday =	🌰 🌰 🌰	**(3)**
Thursday =	🍓 🍓 🍓 🍓	**(4)**
Friday =	🍊 🍊 🍊 🍊 🍊	**(5)**

Example: Monday   (The answer is Tuesday because each Monday
            +Monday   equals one, and 1 + 1 = 2. Tuesday is the day that
            ─────────   matches the number 2.)
            Tuesday

1. Tuesday
   +Wednesday
   ─────────

2. Monday
   +Wednesday
   ─────────

3. Friday
   −Thursday
   ─────────

4. Wednesday
   −Monday
   ─────────

5. Thursday
   −Tuesday
   ─────────

6. Monday
   +Thursday
   ─────────

7. Tuesday
   −Monday
   ─────────

8. Tuesday
   +Monday
   ─────────

9. Friday
   −Tuesday
   ─────────

Bonus: That hungry caterpillar! He ate through a Monday, a Wednesday, and a Friday. What number does that equal in all?

Sorting Saturday

On Saturday, the very hungry caterpillar ate through . . .

. . . 1 piece of chocolate cake

. . . 1 ice-cream cone

. . . 1 pickle

. . . 1 slice of Swiss cheese

. . . 1 slice of salami

. . . 1 lollipop

. . . 1 piece of cherry pie

. . . 1 sausage

. . . 1 cupcake

. . . and 1 slice of watermelon

Sort the foods into their proper food groups.

Dairy	Meat	Fruit	Vegetable	Grains	Snack

Bonus: What other foods can you add to each category? Add one or more to each column.

Number Words and Booklet

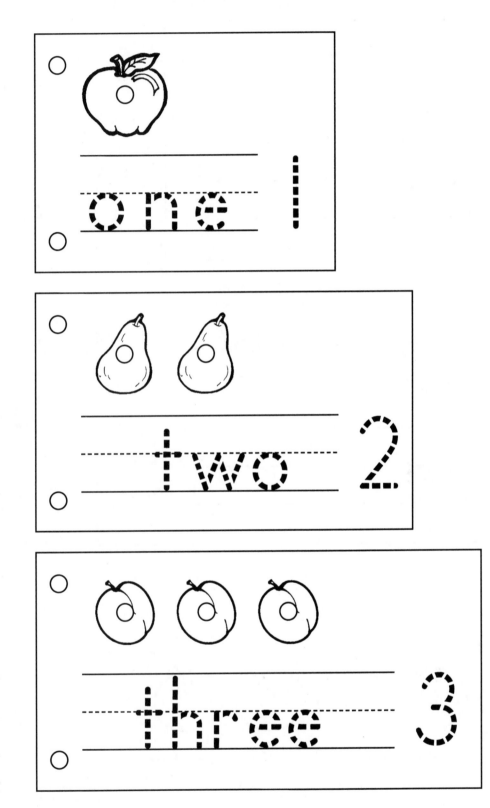

Directions

1. Color and cut out the booklet pages (pages 33–35).

2. Trace the number and number words on each page.

3. Punch the holes on each page. (There are holes on the left side and a hole in each piece of fruit.)

4. Assemble the booklet in number order.

5. Connect the pages by tying with string or yarn through the holes on the left.

6. Once the book is assembled, you will see uniform holes through all the fruit on each page.

7. As you turn each page, weave a chenille stick caterpillar through the holes to see the hungry caterpillar satisfy his appetite!

Number Words and Booklet *(cont.)*

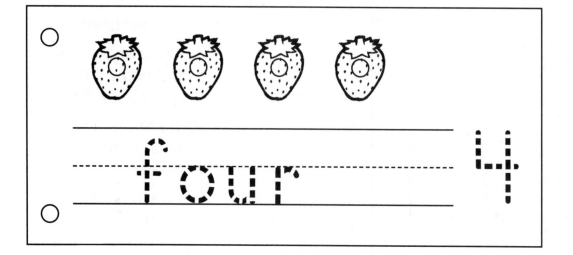

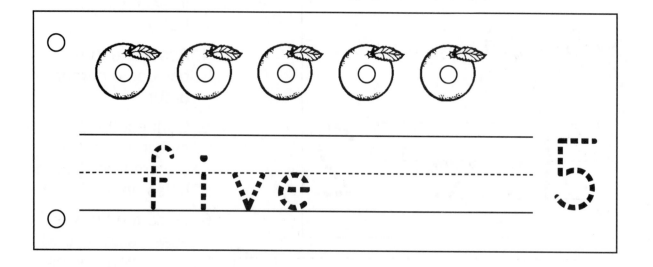

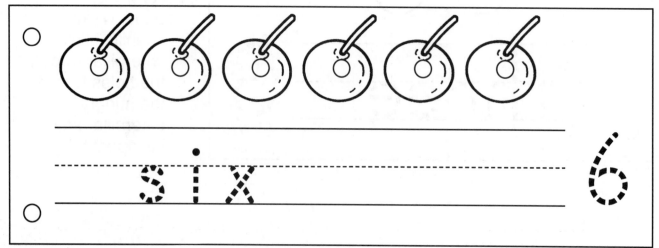

Number Words and Booklet (cont.)

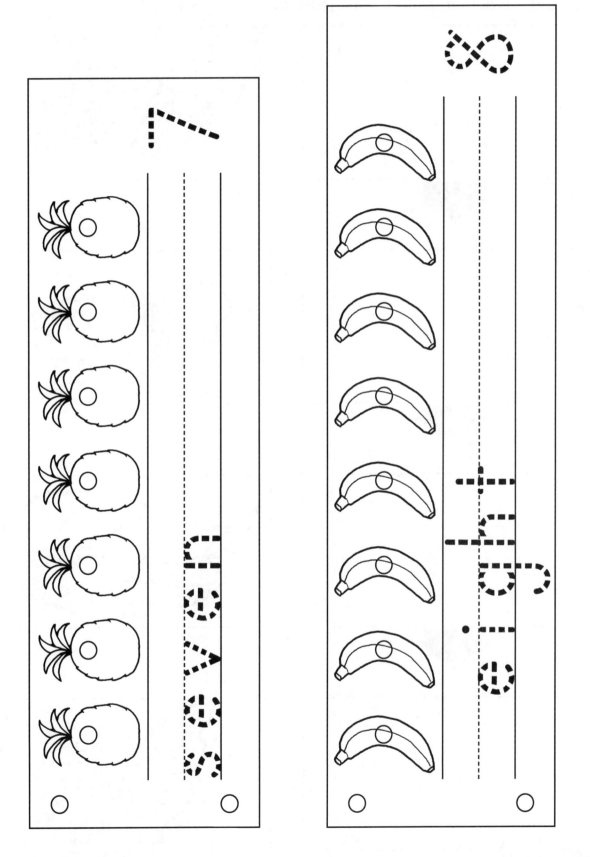

Birth of a Butterfly

Color and cut out the pictures. Glue them in life cycle order.

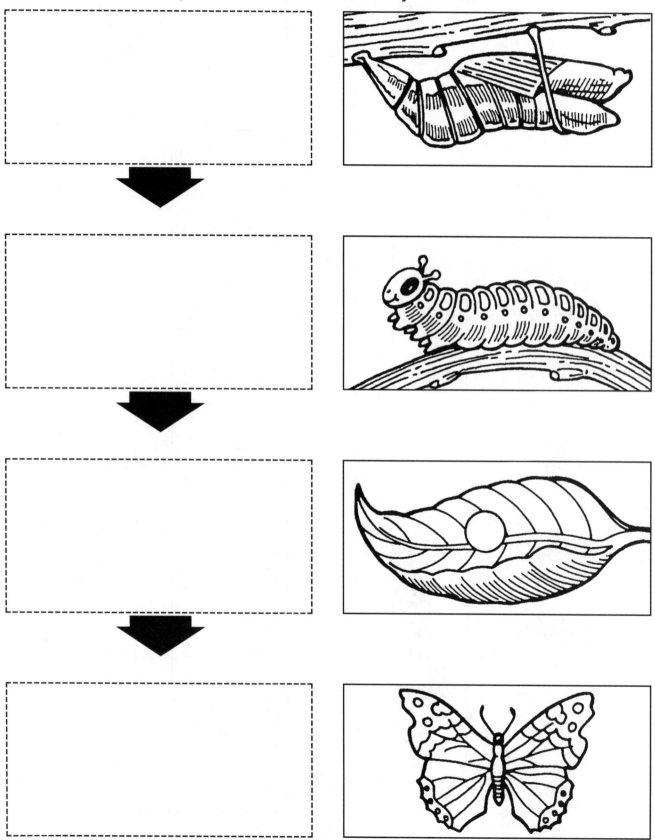

The Very Healthy Caterpillar

What foods do you eat each day?

Do you eat vegetables? _____   Do you eat fruit?_____

Do you eat yogurt? _____   Do you eat cereal? _____

Write the names of other foods you usually eat each day.

_____

_____

_____

_____

It is very important that we eat the right amounts and the right kinds of foods every day. That way we keep our bodies healthy and strong. Study the chart below. It shows the kinds of foods you should eat each day and the number of servings you should have.

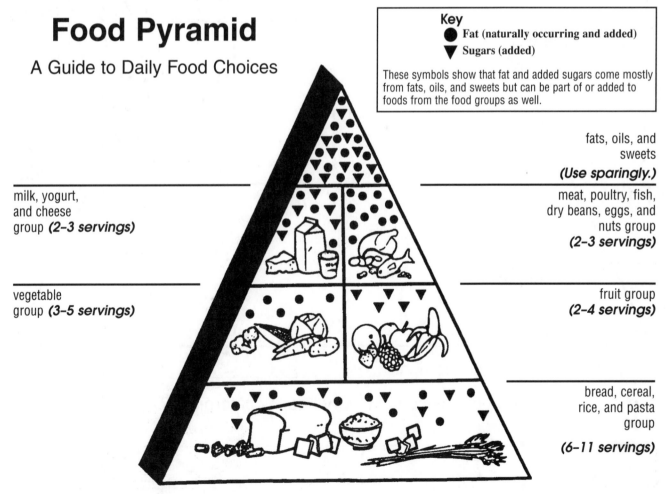

Food Pyramid

A Guide to Daily Food Choices

Key
● Fat (naturally occurring and added)
▼ Sugars (added)

These symbols show that fat and added sugars come mostly from fats, oils, and sweets but can be part of or added to foods from the food groups as well.

milk, yogurt, and cheese group *(2–3 servings)*

vegetable group *(3–5 servings)*

fats, oils, and sweets
(Use sparingly.)

meat, poultry, fish, dry beans, eggs, and nuts group
(2–3 servings)

fruit group
(2–4 servings)

bread, cereal, rice, and pasta group
(6–11 servings)

The Very Healthy Caterpillar *(cont.)*

Fill in the chart on this page with the foods you eat in one day. Be sure to write the foods in the correct sections. Share your chart with your classmates.

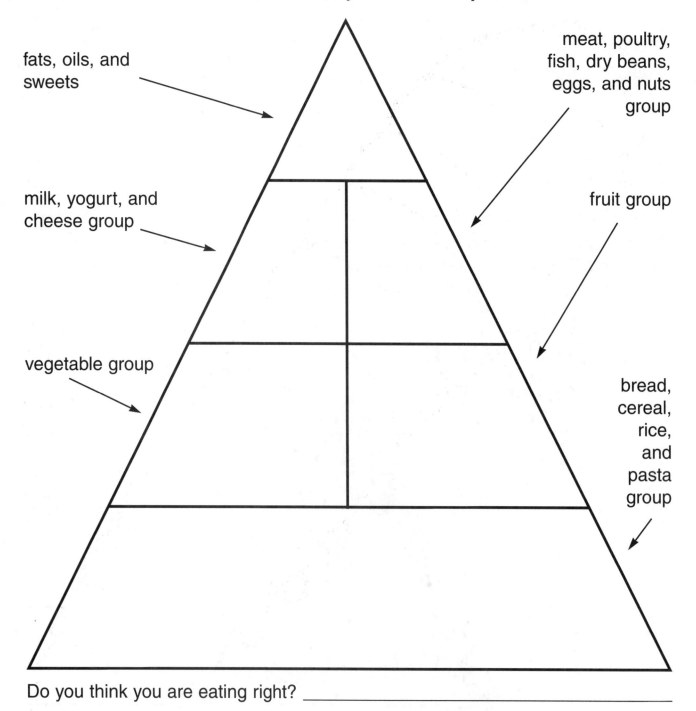

fats, oils, and sweets

meat, poultry, fish, dry beans, eggs, and nuts group

milk, yogurt, and cheese group

fruit group

vegetable group

bread, cereal, rice, and pasta group

Do you think you are eating right? _____

If not, what can you do to become a "very healthy caterpillar"?

_____

_____

Caterpillar Parts

Teacher Note: See page 10 for directions.

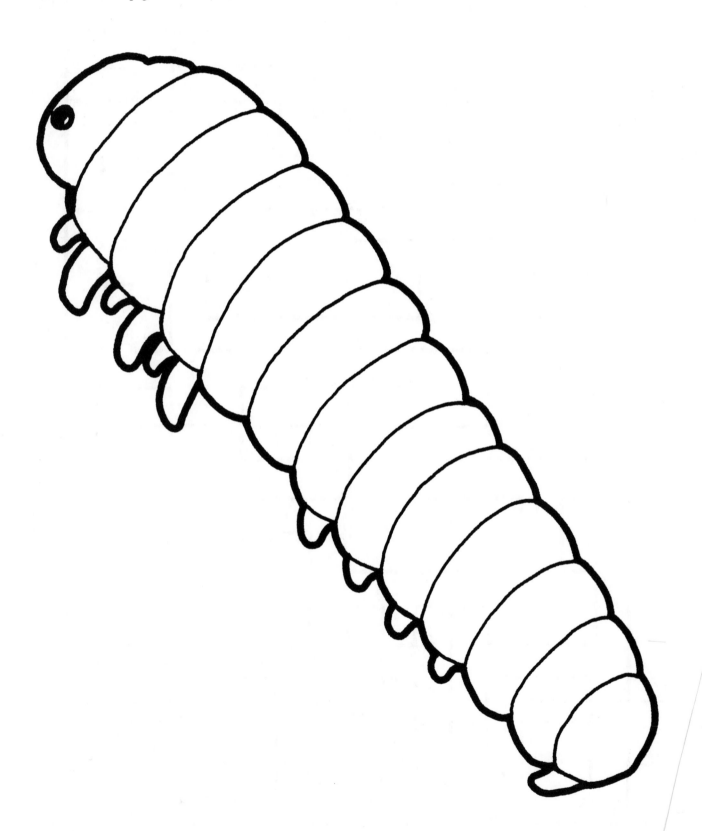

Metamorphosis Maze

Help the caterpillar turn into a butterfly! Follow the maze and color the pictures.

Hungry for Words

Find the words from the story in the word search puzzle.

```
S A T U R D A Y L E A F
T W H C D N N O O C O C
R E U M Y Z P L N S R A
A D N I B B L E D A A T
W N G K N U U X H U N E
B E R Y S T M K S S G R
E S Y Q R T Z G T A E P
R D R P U E Y P G G S I
R A A I A R V Q O E M L
I Y S I E F R I D A Y L
E E U O B L S E L P P A
S U N D A Y P E A R S R
```

caterpillar	Saturday	butterfly	apple	plum
strawberries	Wednesday	oranges	sausage	egg
nibbled	Sunday	Friday	hungry	sun
leaf	cocoon	pears	eat	very

The Very Hungry Caterpillar
Board Game

Teacher Note: See page 11 for directions.

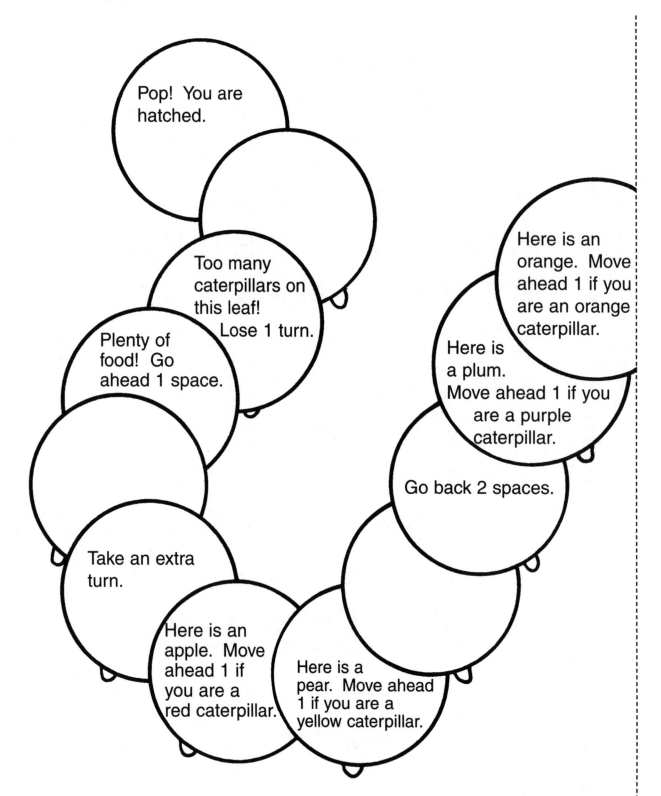

The Very Hungry Caterpillar
Board Game *(cont.)*

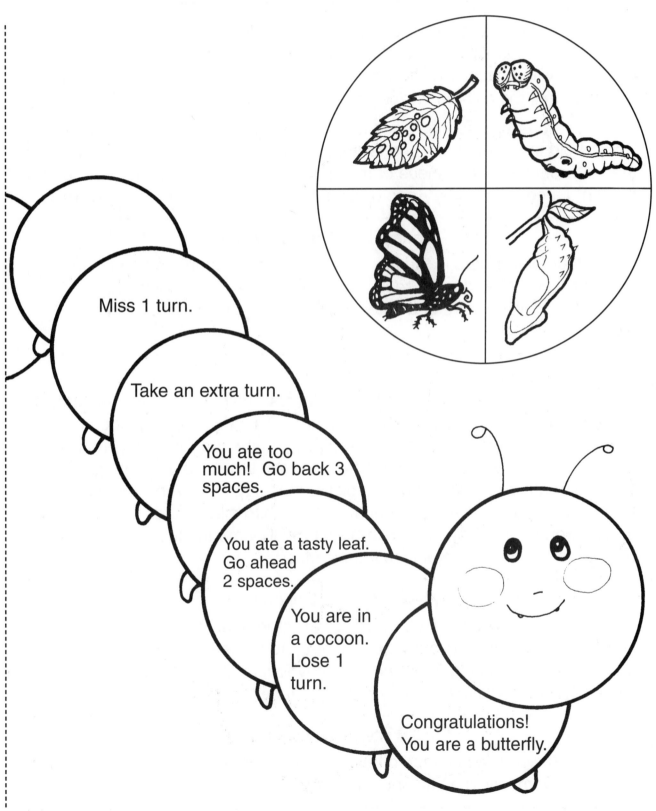

Miss 1 turn.

Take an extra turn.

You ate too much! Go back 3 spaces.

You ate a tasty leaf. Go ahead 2 spaces.

You are in a cocoon. Lose 1 turn.

Congratulations! You are a butterfly.

Caterpillar Center Activities

Teacher Notes: See pages 12 and 45 for directions.

Sponge-Painted Caterpillars and Butterflies

Trace the circle onto different colors of construction paper. Make 13 circles and cut them out. Glue the circles together in one long line. Decorate the end circle with a face. Add antennae cut out of black construction paper. Sponge-paint the colored circles of the caterpillar's body.

To make a butterfly, sponge-paint a half sheet of colored tissue paper and let it dry. Fold the tissue back and forth into a fan. Cut the ends of the fan so they are rounded. Tie a piece of string around the center of the fan. Spread the fan out on both sides. Tape or glue the wings behind the butterfly body.

Caterpillar Observations

Look at the caterpillars in the jar. Observe them through the magnifying glass as well. What do you see? Write down notes about what you observe. Draw a picture of a caterpillar with a lot of detail. Color your picture, too.

Memory Game

Divide into a small group of two to five players. Take turns, one at a time, naming what a hungry caterpillar might eat. (These can be any foods, not just ones that are healthful for a caterpillar.) Name the foods according to the letters of the alphabet. The first player may say, "The Very Hungry Caterpillar ate an apple." The next player may say, "The Very Hungry Caterpillar ate an apple and a banana." The third player adds a *c* food, and so on through the alphabet. Each player must name the foods that came before his or her turn as well as the new food.

Waxed Nature Collections

Take a sheet of waxed paper. Make an arrangement of some of the nature items provided here on your waxed paper. Add a caterpillar cutout. Place another sheet of waxed paper on top. Have an adult help you iron the pieces together to make a pretty nature collage.

Write a New Story

Use the provided work sheet to help you begin an original story about a new creature. Complete the title and then write your story.

Caterpillar Center Activities *(cont.)*

Write a New Story

Now that you know all about *The Very Hungry Caterpillar*, write your own story about another creature that is very . . . ?

The Very_____ _____

by_____ _____

In the light of the moon, a little egg lay on_____.

One_____morning, the warm sun same up and—pop!—out of the

egg came a tiny and very_____ _____.

_____

_____

_____

_____

_____

_____

_____

_____

_____

_____

_____

_____

_____

_____

_____

Caterpillar Feast

To really top off your reading and exploration of *The Very Hungry Caterpillar*, host a Caterpillar Feast. Serve fruit salad and fruit punch. Add leaves for garnish. Invite parents or another class to share your caterpillar treats. Use the invitation below.

At your celebration, you might also consider sharing your original stories, stick puppet plays, and other work you have done throughout this unit. See the bibliography (page 47) for poetry sources in order to offer caterpillar and butterfly recitations.

We made it!

Now we are celebrating, and we want you to come along for our Very Hungry Caterpillar Feast.

When: _____

Where: _____

We will also be sharing our work. Please fly on by to see what we have learned and accomplished!

Bibliography and Related Resources

Other Books by Eric Carle (a partial list)

The Secret Birthday Message. HarperTrophy, 1986
The Very Busy Spider. Philomel Books, 1995
The Very Grouchy Ladybug. HarperCollins, 1996
The Very Lonely Firefly. Putnam Pub Group, 1995
The Very Quiet Cricket. Philomel Books, 1990

Fiction Books

DeLuise, Dom. *Charlie the Caterpillar*. Aladdin Paperbacks, 1993
Fleming, Denise. *In the Tall, Tall Grass*. Henry Holt and Company, 1991
Garelick, May. *Where Does the Butterfly Go When It Rains?* Mondo Publishing, 1997
Kent, Jack. *The Caterpillar and the Polliwog*. Prentice-Hall, 1982
Rippon, Sally. *Cathy Caterpillar and Betty Bee*. Rourke Corporation, 1982
Selsam, Millicent E. *Terry and the Caterpillars*. Harper, 1962
Yep, Lawrence. *Butterfly Boy*. Farrar Straus and Giroux, 1993

Nonfiction Resources

Cohen, Richard. *Snail Trails & Tadpole Tales: Nature Education for Young Children*. Redleaf, 1993
Dorling Kindersley Staff. *Insects and Crawly Creatures*. Macmillan, 1992
Goor, Ron and Nancy. *Insect Metamorphosis: From Egg to Adult*. Macmillan, 1990
Hanks, Dr. Hugh. *The Bug Book and The Bug Bottle*. Workman, 1987
Herberman, Ethan. *The City Kid's Field Guide*. Simon & Schuster, 1989
Oram, Hiawyn. *Creepy Crawly Song Book*. FS & G, 1993
Podendorf, Illa. *Insects*. Children's, 1991
Ransford, Lynn. *Creepy Crawlies for Curious Kids*. Teacher Created Materials, 1987
Royston, Angela. *Insects and Crawly Creatures*. Macmillan, 1992
Sterling, Mary Ellen. *Thematic Unit: Butterflies*. Teacher Created Materials, 1999
Sterling, Mary Ellen. *Thematic Unit: Creepy Crawlies*. Teacher Created Materials, 1990

Poetry

Moss, Jeffrey. *The Butterfly Jar*. Bantam Books, 1989
Rosetti, Christina. "The Caterpillar" in *Sing a Song of Popcorn*. Scholastic, 1988
Rosetti, Christina. "Hurt No Living Thing" in *The Random House Book of Poetry for Children*.
  Random House, 1983
Schulz, Lillian. "Fuzzy Wuzzy, Creepy Crawly" in *Read-Aloud Rhymes for the Very Young*.
  Alfred A. Knopf, 1986
Scollard, Clinton. "The Butterfly" in *Read-Aloud Rhymes for the Very Young*. Alfred A. Knopf, 1986
Shannon, Monica. "Only My Opinion" in *Read-Aloud Rhymes for the Very Young*.
  Alfred A. Knopf, 1986

Insects and Science Equipment

To order caterpillars and other caterpillar paraphernalia for your classroom, call **Insect Lore** at
1-800-LIVE-BUG or contact them on the Internet at www.insectlore.com. Only credit card orders are
taken over the phone or Internet. Otherwise, request a catalog. Write to the company at P.O. Box
1535, Shafter, CA 93263. Please be aware that bugs are available at only certain times of the year.

Answer Key

page 27

1. caterpillar
2. egg
3. Monday, Friday, Sunday
4. Wednesday
5. Answers will vary.

page 28

I.

1. cupcake, lollipop, pickle
2. ate, caterpillar, watermelon
3. Friday, Saturday, Thursday
4. caterpillar, cocoon, cupcake

II.

1. sausage
2. caterpillar
3. cocoon
4. hungry
5. butterfly

III. Answers will vary. Possible words include *cat, pill, are, ate, pile, pail, tea, at, art, apt, plate, trace, ace, rat, pat, trail, crate, rate.*

page 29

1. warm, egg, caterpillar
2. Monday, apple, hungry
3. five
4. night, stomachache
5. cocoon
6. two
7. hole
8. butterfly

page 31

1. Friday
2. Thursday
3. Monday
4. Tuesday
5. Tuesday
6. Friday
7. Monday
8. Wednesday
9. Wednesday
   Bonus: 9

page 36

egg on leaf, caterpillar, cocoon, butterfly

page 40

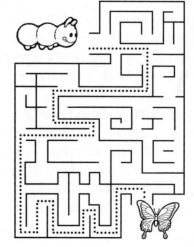

page 41